Carolina Friends School
Durham Early School

Photographed by DORKA RAYNOR

This Is My Father and Me

Albert Whitman & Company, Chicago

Werd'ich zum Augenblicke sagen:
Verweile doch!
Du bist so shoen!

Life's fleeting moment —
Linger a while!
Thou art so fair!
            —from Goethe's Faust

This book is for my father, Lazar Funt

Library of Congress Cataloging in Publication Data
Raynor, Dorka, 1916-
  This is my father and me.
  SUMMARY: Photographs (accompanied by brief captions)
record the activities of fathers and their children in
many different countries.
  1. Father and child — Pictorial works — Juvenile
literature. [1. Family — Pictures and illustrations.
2. Father and child — Pictures and illustrations]
  I. Title
HQ756.R38   310.42'7   73-7320
ISBN 0-8075-7883-5
Second Printing 1978
Copyright © 1973 by Dorka Raynor
Published simultaneously in Canada by
George J. McLeod, Limited, Toronto
All rights reserved. Printed in U.S.A.

1 A temple courtyard, Tokyo, Japan

2 Airport, Miami, U.S.A.

3 The market in Santo Domingo de los Colorados, Ecuador

4 Temple, Bali, Indonesia

A pilgrimage to the Basilica of Our Lady of Guadalupe, Mexico City, Mexico

7 Lincoln Park, Chicago, U.S.A.

At the Mediterranean, Djerba, Tunisia

8 Central Park, New York City, U.S.A.

11 Italian city square

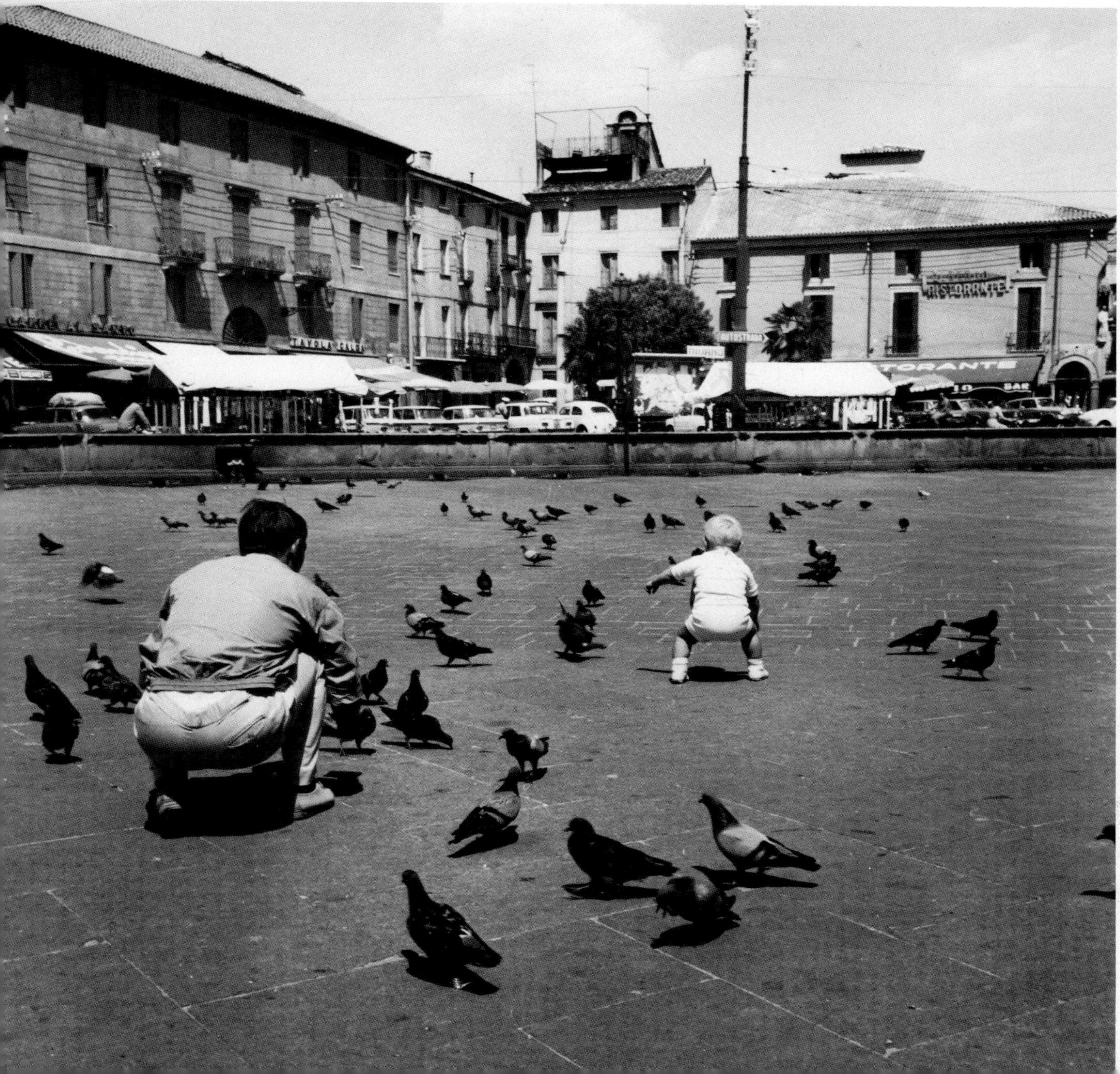

12 A policeman in Vila Real, Portugal

15 Eastertime, at the zoo, Chicago, U.S.A.

16 Amusement park, Vienna, Austria

18 Brandenburg Gate, East Berlin, Germany

19 Three on a scale at Honfleur, France

20 Charleroi, Belgium

21 Bazaar, Isfahan, Ira

22 Spring, Andalusia, Spain

23 Otavalo, Ecuador

24 A safe ride for a Tunisian boy

25 On the way to the temple, Bali, Indonesia

26 Market, Chichicastenango, Guatemala

27 A haircut, Katmandu, Nepal

28 Chinese fisherman, Hong Kong

30
Muhammad's
birthday,
Penang, Federati
of Malaysia

3
Market, Otavalo
Ecuador

32 Musicians at a shrine, Nepal

33 Colorado Indians, Santo Domingo de los Colorados, Ecuador

34 Village festival, Sakamoto, Japan

35 At prayer, Bali, Indonesia

36 Taipei, Taiwan (Formosa)

37 At home, U.S.A.

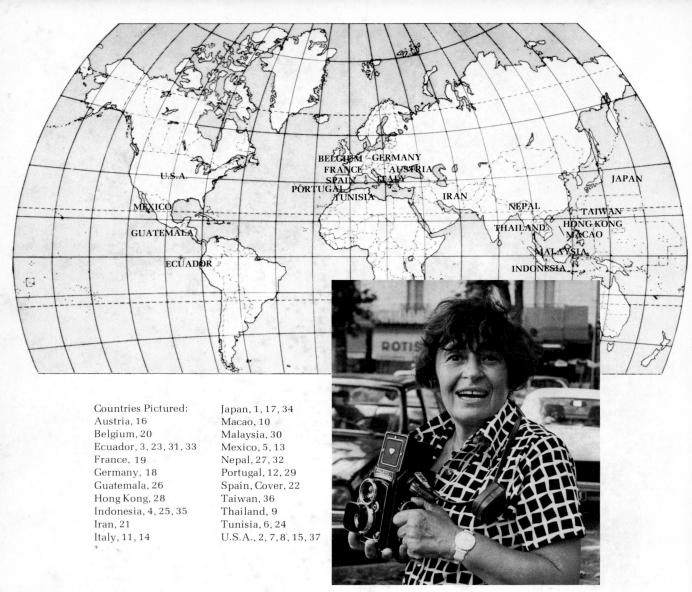

DORKA RAYNOR is internationally known for her photographs of children. Curator of prints and drawings at the Metropolitan Museum of Art, in New York, A. Hyatt Mayor has said, "Mrs. Raynor's human and distinguished photographs strike a note that is all her own and that add to the richness and variety of photography today." In addition to having prints in leading collections, Mrs. Raynor has been honored by the American Society of Magazine Photographers and has won prizes in France and Japan.

Mrs. Raynor, who lives in Winnetka, Illinois, was born in Warsaw, Poland. When a bride she went to Barcelona, Spain, as a photographer and journalist. In 1938 she and her husband, Professor Severin Raynor of Northwestern University, came to the United States. The Raynors travel frequently, and always Mrs. Raynor's Rolleiflex is ready for the glimpse that is revealing or poignant.